I0493767

TABLE OF CONTENTS

Star Power - Using Celebrities for Interviews & Promotions
How to Use Celebrity Endorsements and Where to Find & Contact Celebrities
©Copyright 2013 by Dr. Leland Benton

DISCLAIMER AND TERMS OF USE AGREEMENT:

(Please Read This Before Using This Book)

educational purposes. Therefore, if you wish to apply ideas contained in this book, you are taking full responsibility for your actions.

The author and publisher disclaim any warranties (express or implied), merchantability, or fitness for any particular purpose. The author and publisher shall in no event be held liable to any party for any direct, indirect, punitive, special, incidental or other consequential damages arising directly or indirectly from any use of this material, which is provided "as is", and without warranties. As always, the advice of a competent legal, tax, accounting, medical or other professional should be sought where applicable.

The author and publisher do not warrant the performance, effectiveness or applicability of any sites listed or linked to in this book. All links are for information purposes only and are not warranted for content, accuracy or any other implied or explicit purpose. No part of this may be copied, or changed in any format, or used in any way other than what is outlined within this course under any circumstances. Violators will be prosecuted.

This book is © Copyrighted by ePubWealth.com.

In writing this book, my goal is to provide a concise business resource for my reader as well as correct and pertinent information regarding celebrity endorsements.

There is a good deal of "false" information out there and information that is downright misleading. Using celebrities for endorsements, interviews, etc. is something that needs to be well thought out including putting together a business plan-type document that outlines everything you need in order to succeed.

I am the Editor-in-Chief of an international publishing house called ePubWealrh.com and although I know a good many celebrities by their first names, I very rarely engage them for my contract author's books. The reason being is that I look to see if the "Star Power" matches the cost. In other words, am I going to sell enough books to pay for the celebrity endorsement and will this endorsement make a difference in my book sales.

Every product is different because every product has a different price point and gross profit. Books do not have high price points or gross profits so care is needed in evaluating a celebrity endorsement.

I know it looks "cool" having a celebrity endorse your "stuff" but looking at it purely from a business standpoint is necessary for profitability.

This book is one in my series of business resources:

Business Resources

21st Century Marketing Genius
http://www.amazon.com/dp/B008A07WBW
Body Language
http://www.amazon.com/dp/B006INI18G
Body Talk
http://www.amazon.com/dp/B0079MA1XS
Copyright Law Guidebook
http://www.amazon.com/dpB00BHEYBK8
Cyber Protect Your Business
http://www.amazon.com/dp/B0095JEAYY
Distraction Marketing
http://www.amazon.com/dp/B006IUVBWM
Distraction Video Marketing
http://www.amazon.com/dp/B00BURDLAI
Effective Email Advertising
http://www.amazon.com/dp/B006IV2300
Fast TV EXPOSURE
http://www.amazon.com/dp/B00939A1YY
Gender Differences in Advertising
http://www.amazon.com/dp/B006IOCG9U

Investment Phrases
http://www.amazon.com/dp/B008LO3Y00
International Standard Book Numbers
http://www.amazon.com/dp/B00B2YB4SK
Latin Phrases
http://www.amazon.com/dp/B006ITY7TW
Legal Phrases
http://www.amazon.com/dp/B008LOA0Q6
Real Estate Phrases
http://www.amazon.com/dp/B008LQ7BMK
Predictable Advertising
http://www.amazon.com/dp/B00B0SWNPG
The Postcarders
http://www.amazon.com/dp/B006IUUV6O
The Power of Concentration
http://www.barnesandnoble.com/w/the-power-of-concentration-dr-harry-jay/1114037587?ean=2940016133140
The Power of Focus & Application
http://www.barnesandnoble.com/w/the-power-of-focus-application-dr-leland-benton/1046480344?ean=2940016459745
The Power of Observation
http://www.amazon.com/dp/B006IU99EY
The Power of Trained Observation
http://www.amazon.com/dp/B00BSRYMGW
The Psychology of Sales
http://www.amazon.com/dp/B006IUH0GI
The Publishing Agreement
http://www.amazon.com/dp/B00BKGTQZI
Triggers That Cause Buyers to Open Their Wallets
http://www.amazon.com/dp/B00ASWOT7K
Viral Image Marketing

My goal is to provide my readers with information they can't obtain elsewhere and in my 32-years of being a publisher and author, I have found that business resources that address certain subjects in detail are the ones I use the most.

In many cases, upon close examination and analysis, it isn't profitable to use certain resources that are available for advertising and promotion. Why waste good money?

In this book I want my readers to carefully analyze if celebrity endorsements can be profitable for whatever product they are advertising and promoting. Celebrity endorsements are very effective when used properly but just as ineffective if used wrongfully. This book will assist you in your evaluations.

Like I stated previously, I know many celebrities by their first names and can easily pick up the phone and talk to them but with that said I am very discriminating in using celebrities. I want you to think outside the box from the traditional use of celebrity endorsements.

For example, one of the super effective ways to use celebrities is in a "meetup" environment. I often rent a ballroom in a major hotel and major city and invite my authors and readers to a meetup. I also invite at least three to six celebrities to come out and mingle with my guests. I provide wine and cheese and the setting is casual and social. In the rear of the ballroom I set up a small book store with my author's books, videos, audiobooks, etc. These meetups have been very successful with my last one in Las Vegas drawing over 2,000 guests.

Think outside the box when using celebrity endorsements!! I will be offering more examples of this as you go through this book just to give you some ideas. Feel free to use them and if you have any questions please write to me: lee.benton@epubwealth.com.

Okay, let's get at the good stuff…

Chapter 1 – Star Power Publicity: The Power of Celebrity Endorsement

Star Power Publicity is a super effective way to get your product or service known to the general public while at the same time providing an effective branding tool for the same product/service.

Here are some things to consider when evaluating using celebrity endorsements:

1. **Matching the Celebrity to Your Product/Service** – you would use Angeline Jolie (BTW –she rarely does endorsements) or Jennifer Aniston (she does) to sell a carburetor. That is silly! Matching the star to your product/service is very important and once you move to engage a celebrity you will see that it is very important to them too. BIG NOTE: each star's representatives will check out you, your company, your product/service, just about everything before they

even consider your request. They will make sure you have insurance, a hold harmless agreement, and the ability to pay, etc before they begin serious discussions with you.

2. **Cost of Campaign** – Analyzing ALL of the costs of a campaign where you will be using celebrity endorsements is essential. Using my meetups that I described in the Introduction as an example, my costs included, advertising the event, renting the hotel ballroom, food service per attendee, cost of the celebrities, which included airfare and hotel accommodations, cost of my staff that attended the event with me including food, airfare and hotel accommodations, cost of setting up the bookstore – transportation, bookstore display, etc, insurance, and more. This stuff isn't cheap but with over 2,000 attendees, it was profitable but barely. The goodwill and branding aspect cannot be calculated in dollars and cents but this is where the true value came into play. My attendees got a chance to meet the authors, the celebrities, take pictures, socialize, have some cheese and wine and they bought a ton of books and products too.

3. **Advertising & Promoting Your Event** – it doesn't matter if you use the meetup scenario outlined above or whatever scenario you use while engaging celebrity endorsements, you must advertise and promote your event and this aspect needs very special attention. In all of my events I use television and email marketing to obtain my attendees. I have found this to be most effective.

Two of my business resource books listed in the Introduction are "Effective Email Advertising" and "Fast TV Exposure," where I discuss in detail using these two types of advertising and promotion. BTW – both of these two programs are an essential element in factoring your costs.

4. **Publicity for Your Event or Promotion** – no matter what type of event or promotion you are planning, you need publicity to get it out there. Here is a very extensive twitter directory, which will enable you to send a #hashtag message to its recipients:

PR News' Twitter Directory

Name	Title	Twitter Handle
PR News		@PRNews
Steve Goldstein	Editorial Director, Events	@SGoldsteinAI
Sreyashi Kanjilal	Conference Content Associate	@s_kanjilal
Bill Miltenberg	Community Editor	@bmiltenberg
Charlie Sands	Director, Web Development	@charliesands
Kate Schaeffer	Director of Event Logistics & Marketing	@k8schaeffer
Diane Schwartz	Senior Vice President & Group Publisher	@dianeschwartz
Matthew Schwartz	Group Editor	@mpsjourno1

Laura Snitkovskiy	Marketing Manager	@LauraEBerd
Amy Urban-Jefferies	Associate Publisher & Brand Director	@aujefferies
Scott Van Camp	Editor	@svancamp01

PR AGENCIES & CONSULTANTS

Name	Twitter Handle
4GreenPs	@4GreenPs
5W Public Relations	@5W_PR
The 10 Company	@the10company
A F Prince Associates	@princeportfolio
Abbott Public Relations	@nhprman
Access Communications	@AccessPR
Acuity Public Relations LLC	@AcuityPR
Acumen	@acumenpr
Advantis Communications	@AdvantisComm
AEOM PR	@AEOMPR
Affect Strategies	@TeamAffect
Airfoil PR	@airfoilpr
Allison & Partners	@AllisonPR
Altimeter Group	@altimetergroup
AMP Agency	@AMP_Agency
Amy Sutnick Plotch Communications	@amyplotch

12

Andonia Public Relations	@AndoniaPR
Anton Communications	@antonprtweets
Anvil Media Inc.	@anvilmedia
APCO Worldwide	@apcoworldwide
Aqua Communications	@aquacommpr
Archer>Malmo PR	@archomalmopr
Arieff Communications	@arieffcomm
Arketi Group	@Arketi
AR|PR	@ar_pr
Atomic PR	@AtomicPR
Auritt Communications Group	@aurittcomms
Authentic PR	@Authentic_PR
Awesome Communications, Ltd.	@AwesomeComms
AxiCom	@axicomUS
Babel PR	@BabelPR
Bay & Associates	@baytalks
BBDO	@BBDOWorldwide
Be Bold Media	@beboldpr
Be Social Public Relations	@BeSocialPR
Beckerman PR	@BeckermanPR
Beehive PR	@beehivepr
Bender/Helper Impact	@BHImpact
Berman and Co.	@BermanCo
Big Click Syndicate	@godvertiser
BIM Communications	@BIM_COMM
Black Twig Communications	@BlackTwigPR
Bliss PR	@BlissPR
Bluewood Training	@BluewoodTra

BlueIvyCommunications	@BlueIvyCommin
BookSparksPR	@BookSparksPR
Booz Allen Hamilton	@BoozAllen
Brandware	@BrandwarePR
Bread and Butter PR	@BBPR
Brodeur Partners	@BrodeurPartners
Brown-Miller Communications	@BrownMillerPR
Brownstein Group	@brownstein_grp
Buddy Media	@BuddyMedia
Burke Communications	@BurkeCom
BurrellesLuce	@BurrellesLuce
Burson-Marsteller	@BMGlobalNews
Burson-Marsteller Sweden	@BMse
Burson-Marsteller United Kingdom	@BMUKNews
Business Wire	@Businesswire
Calypso Communications	@calypsotweet
Capstrat	@capstrat
CARMA International	@CARMA_Tweets
Carmichael Lynch Spong	@cl_spong
The Castle Group	@CastleGRP
Catalyst Public Relations	@PRCatalyst
Cavenger Agency	@cavengeragency
Cercone Brown	@CerconeBrown

Cerrell Associates	@CerrellAssoc
CFA	@cfamarketing
Chaffin Communications, Inc	@chaffinoutdoors
Change Matters	@changemtrs
Cision	@cision
Civic Entertainment Group	@CEGNY
Clarity Solutions	@MediaClarity
Clearpoint Agency	@ClearpointPR
Cliqstudios.com	@cliqstudios
Co+Co	@comcontrp
Cognito	@cognitopr
Cohn & Wolfe	@cohnwolfe
Cohn Marketing	@CohnMarketing
Communications Strategies	@Cstratinc
CommunicationWorks, LLC	@CommWorksLLC
Cone Inc.	@ConeLLC
Conover Tuttle Pace	@ctpboston
The Content Factory	@ContentFAC
Cookerly Public Relations	@CookerlyPR
Copy Creators	@Copy_Creators
Coyne PR	@coynepr
Creating Results	@CreatingResults
Creative Alliance Communications	@AileenRSchlef
Crenshaw Communications	@crenshawcomm
Crescendo Communications	@crescendocollab

Crier Communications	@crierpr
Crosby Marketing Communications	@CrosbyMarketing
Crossroads Public Relations	@crossroadspr
CRT/tanaka	@crttanaka
Cubitt Jacobs & Prosek Communications	@CJPcom
Culp & Co.	@Culpwrit
Davies	@DaviesPA
Davies Murphy Group	@daviesmurphy
Delcass Communications	@delcass
Derek Mooney Communications	@dsmooney
Development Counsellors International	@AboutDCI
Deveney Communication	@deveneynola
DeVries Public Relations	@DeVriesPR
DHR Communications	@DHRComms
DIALOGO	@dialogopr
Digital Kitchen	@digitalkitchen
Dodge Communications	@DodgeComm
Drummer PR	@DrummerPR
DSM Communications	@DSM_Com
DVStrategies LLC	@DVStrategies
Dye, Van Mol & Lawrence	@pradicalblog
Edelman PR	@EdelmanPR
The Elevatyd Experience Group	@Elevatyd
Engage121	@engage121
Entrinsiq	@entrinsiq
Epic PR Group	@EpicPRGroupDC
Euro RSCG Worldwide	@EuroRSCG
Expion	@Expion
Fahlgren Mortine Public Relations	@FahlgrenMort

	ine
Fast Horse	@Fast_Horse
Faye Clack Communications	@FayeClack
Fineman PR	@FinemanPR
First and Last PR	@firstandlastPR
Fleishman-Hillard	@Fleishman
FMC Technologies	@FMC_Tech
FoodMinds	@FoodMinds
Fraser Communications	@frasercom
French | West | Vaughn	@FWV_US
Fresh Image PR	@FreshImagePR
Frost & Sullivan	@frost_sullivan
Full Circle PR	@FullCircle_PR
Fuguet Comunicacion y Cambio	@Fuguetcom
Gambel Communications	@GambelPR
Geben Communication	@gebencomm
Geelmuyden-Kiese	@GeelmuydenKiese
get noticed! communications	@getnoticed_de
Gibbs & Soell Inc.	@gibbs_soell
Gibraltar Associates	@GibraltarAssoc
Gnosis Media Group	@gnosisarts
Golin Harris	@GolinHarris
Golin Harris Sweden	@GolinHarrisSWE
Golin Harris Texas	@GolinHarrisTX
Golin Harris United Kingdom	@GolinHarrisUK
Goodby, Silverstein & Partners	@GSP

Grand Central Marketing	@GCMMatthew
Grasshopper Group	@GHGroup
Gravitas Communications	@GravitasComm
The Greensheet	@thegreensheet
Gregory FCA Communications	@GregoryFCA
GroundFloor Media	@GroundFloorPR
GYMR	@GYMRPR
gyro	@gyro
H&M Communications	@hm_comm
Hager Sharp, Inc.	@hagersharp
Hamptons Creative Group	@HamptonsCG
Henman Communications, Ltd.	@HenmanComm
Henson Consulting	@hensonconsult
High Road Communications	@WeAreHighRoad
Hill & Knowlton	@hillandknowlton
Hispanicize	@hispanicize
HMA Public Relations	@HMA_PR
H&M Communications	@hm_comm
The Hoffman Agency	@DailyBrew
Hotwood PR	@hopwoodpr
Horn Group	@horngroup
Hotwire PR	@HotwirePR
Howard Merrell & Partners	@hmandp
Humanability	@humanabilityusa
Hunter Public Relations	@HunterPR

idreamSpeakers	@idreamspeakers
ICR	@ICRPR
ignition	@ignitioninc
Imelda Dulcich Public Relations	@ImeldaDulcichPR
IMJ Communications, LLC	@imjcomm
Impassion Media	@impassionmedia
Impress Labs	@ImpressTweets
The In-House Writer	@inhousewriter
InkHouse Media + Marketing	@inkhousepr
Integrate PR	@IntegratePR
Integrated PR	@Integrated_PR
Interkom	@Interkominc
iostudio	@iostudio
J Group Media	@JGroupMedia
JSH&A	@JSHAPR
J. Walter Thompson Advertising	@JWT_Worldwide
Jackson Spalding	@jacksonspalding
Jaffe PR	@JAFFE_PR
Jasculca Terman & Associates	@JasculcaTerman
JCPR, Inc.	@JCPR
The Jeffrey Group	@TheJeffreyGroup
JEM PR & Communications	@jem_pr
Jones Public Relations	@jonesprinc
Juniper Networks	@JuniperNetwo

	rks
Kaleidoscope Media	@kaleidoscopepr
Kaplow PR	@kaplowpr
Karson Communications	@karsoncommunications
Katcher Vaughn & Bailey Public Relations	@KVBPR
Kaya Media Strategies	@kayamedia
Ketchum	@KetchumPR
Kitchen Public Relations	@KitchenPRNYC
Knock on Wood Communications	@kowpr
Kohnstamm Communications	@Kohnstamm
Lambert, Edwards & Associates	@LambertEdwards
Landis Communications	@LandisComm
Lane PR	@LANEPR
LAPR	@LAPRAGENCY
LaunchSquad	@LaunchSquad
Laurie Pehar Borsh PR	@LPBPR
LawFirmsPR	@LawFirmsPR
LeadDog Marketing	@atLeadDog
Lewis PR	@lewisprus
Liggett Stashower	@buildingbrands
Linhart Public Relations	@LinhartPR
Link Positive, Inc.	@LinkPositive
Lippe Taylor Brand Communications	@LippeTaylor
Live in Five Public Relations	@liveinfivepr
Lou Hammond & Associates	@LouHammon

20

	dPR
lotus823	@lotus823
LR Consulting Enterprise	@LRConsultingENT
M5 Agency	@m5agencyaz
Madison+Main	@madisonmain
Madison Worldwide	@madisonworldwide
Makeover Media	@makeovermedia
Makovsky + Company	@makovsky
March Communications	@marchpr
The Marcus Group	@MarcusGroup
Marina Maher Communications	@MMCtweets
The Market Council	@marketcouncil
Marketwire	@Marketwire
Markowitz Communications	@MarkowitzComm
Maroon PR	@maroonpr
Matter Communications	@MatterComm
mBLAST	@mBLAST
M/C/C	@mccpr
McNeely Pigott & Fox	@mpfpr
McDougall Travers Collins	@McDougallTC
McKim Cringan George	@mckimcg
MCS Healthcare PR	@MCSHealthcarePR
Mediacom	@MediaComGlobal
Merritt Group	@MerrittGroup
Middleberg Communications	@MiddlebergP

	R
Miller Meiers Design for Communication	@millermeiers
millerrupp	@millerrupp
Mindful Kreative	@MindfulKreative
Mirror Communications	@mirror_comms
Momentum PR	@mprcc
Moonlight Media Ltd.	@MoonlightPR
Moore Consulting Group	@MooreConsulting
Moroch Partners	@MorochPartners
Motion Marketing & Media	@m3_group
MSL Group	@msl_group
Mulberry Marketing Communications	@mulberryglobal
MWW Group	@MWWGroup
Mynewsdesk	@mynewsdesk
Mynt Public Relations	@MyntPR
Nancy J. Friedman PR	@NJFPR
NATIONAL Public Relations	@NATIONALPR
neonFROG	@msneonfrog
Newsmaker Group	@NMGPR
NicheValue Creative Group	@NcVanderhall
North 6th Agency	@North6thAgency
Ogilvy PR Worldwide	@OgilvyPR
O'Malley Hansen	@OmalleyHansen
OpenSpan	@openspan

Overdrive Interactive	@ovrdrv
Pace & Partners, Inc.	@PaceandPartners
Padilla Speer Beardsley	@padilla_psbpr
PainePR	@Paine_PR
Pan Communications	@PANcomm
Panorama Public Relations	@PPR
Parker Hannifin - SSD Drives Div.	@ParkerSSD
Peppercom	@Peppercom
Peritus	@Perituspr
PerkettPR	@PerkettPR
The Phelps Group	@thephelpsgroup
Pierpont Communications	@PierpontCom
Pink & White Consulting LLP	@pwcpr
Pipitone Group	@PipitoneGroup
The Pita Group	@PitaGroup
PIVOT	@PIVOTpr
The Placemaking Group	@placemaking
POP! pr + events	@POPpr_events
Porter Novelli	@porternovelli
Porter Novelli	@PN_ATX
Porter Novelli	@PNIQ
PowerImage Public Relations	@powerimagepr
PR.com	@prcom
PR Focused	@prfocused
PR Newswire	@PRNewswire
PR WIRE	@prwiresl
pr-online.com	@pr_online_com

Primum Marketing Communications	@Primum
Pro Motion Inc.	@ProMotionInc
ProActive Communications	@ProActiveComm
Cognito	@cognitoPR
Profiles, Inc.	@ProfilesBmore
Protiviti	@Protiviti
PRWeb	@prweb
Public Communications Worldwide	@globalprtrends
Purrfect PR	@PurrfectPR
Qorvis Communications	@qorvis
The Quell Group	@thequellgroup
Quinn & Company	@Quinnandco
Racepoint Group	@racepointgroup
Radian6	@Radian6
Rasky Baerlein Strategic Communications	@RaskyBaerlein
R&J Public Relations	@randjpr
rbb PR	@rbbPR
RED PR	@REDPRnyc
Red Public Relations	@redpr
Red Tile PR	@redtilepr
Regan Communications Group	@ReganComm
Renomme Communication	@RenommeGroup
Requiem Media	@requiem_NYC
Revive PR	@RevivePR
Right Service	@rightservice

Ritter Public Relations	@RitterPR
Ritz Communications	@ritzcomms
RL PR & Marketing	@RLPR09
Roadrunner Talent and Media	@RoadrunnerTalen
Rubberneck Media	@RubberneckMedia
Ruder Finn	@RuderFinn
Russia PR News	@ru_pr
The Safdar Group	@ShabbirSafdar
SalesBlend	@SalesBlend
Saxum	@Saxum_US
SBC Advertising	@SBCAdvertising
Schneider Associates	@SchneiderPR
Schwartz Communications	@schwartzcomm
Schwartz Media Strategies	@schwartzmedia
SearchPR	@SearchPR
Seigenthaler PR	@SeigenthalerPR
Shank Public Relations Counselors, Inc.	@Shank_PR
Sharp Consulting Group	@sharpconsults
Shift Consulting	@ShiftConsultant
Shirley & Banister Public Affairs	@sbpublicaffairs
Shoestring Group	@ShoestringGroup
Simantel Group	@simantel

Simply PR	@simplypr
Sixfold Media	@sixfoldmedia
The Skills Group	@skillstracker
Snap Design	@snapsays
SocialChorus	@SocialChorus
Solomon McCown & Co.	@solomonmccown
Solomon McCown & Co.	@HealthBostonPR
Solomon McCown & Co.	@REBostonPR
Solomon McCown & Co.	@CorpBostonPR
Solomon McCown & Co.	@CrisisBostonPR
Solomon McCown & Co.	@MissionBostonPR
Somersault Group	@smrsault
Sonnhalter	@SonnhalterB2T
SOWEB Inc.	@sowebinc
SparkPoint Studio	@SparkPointTeam
SparkPR	@Spark_PR
SpecOps Comm	@SpecOpsComm
Spectrum Media	@smwdc
Spotlight Communications	@spotlight535
SPPR Consultants	@spprconsultants
Sprig Social Media	@sprigsocial
SS	PR	@sspr
Standing Partnership	@standingpr
Step Ahead, Inc.	@StepAheadInc

Sterling Cross Communications	@SterlingCrossPR
Stern + Associates	@sternassociates
Straight Talk Group	@straighttalkpr
StrategicAmpersand	@StratAmp
Susan Magrino Agency	@SMAPR
Sweeney PR	@SweeneyPR
T Chisholm Communications	@tchisholmcomm
Tartaglia Communications	@TartagliaComm
Taylor Strategy	@taylorstrategy
Tene Nicole	@TeneNicolePR
Text 100 Global PR	@text100
Tierney	@hellotierney
t!psPR	@tpsPR
Tipton Communications	TiptonCom
TMG Brand Communications	@TMG_Branding_PR
Torchia Communications	@TorchiaCom
ToyBox Consulting	@toybox206
Travers Collins	@TraversCollins
TrendSide PR	@TrendSide_PR
Trompeter Government Relations & Support Services	@LobbyChampion
T.Y. Lin International	@tyli_group
Vault Communications	@VaultComm
Venture Growth, LLC	@VentureGrowth

Version 2.0 Communications	@v2comms
Vest Advertising	@Vestadvertising
Via Marketing	@Via_Marketing
VINE COMMUNICATIONS	@vinePR
VMS	@VMSVoice
Vocus	@VocusPR
Vollmer Public Relations	@vollmerpr
VOXUS, Inc.	@VoxusPR
Waggener Edstrom	@waggeneredstrom
Waggener Edstrom Corporate Citizenship	@WE_Citizen
Waggener Edstrom Crisis Comms	@WE_CrisisComms
Waggener Edstrom Digital Comms	@WEStudioD
Waggener Edstrom Germany	@Wemunich
Waggener Edstrom Hong Kong	@WaggedHK
Waggener Edstrom South Africa	@WEJoburg
Waggener Edstrom TV	@WE_TV
Waggener Edstrom UK	@WE_UK
WCG	@WCGWorld
Weber Shandwick	@webershandwick
Weber Shandwick Asia Pacific	@1webershandwick
Weber Shandwick North	@WS_North
Weidert Group	@WeidertGroup
Weise Communications	@Weise_Ideas
Wendy Van Parys Marketing Communications	@wvpmc

The Whole Enchilada PR	@WholEnchiladaPR
Widmeyer Communications	@WidmeyerComms
William Mills Agency	@wmagency
Williamson and Williams	@WandWPR
WMG Promotions	@wmgpromotions
Woblee Social Marketing Services	@wobbleee
Wolfstar	@WolfstarPR
Word of Art	@WordArtSG
Working Dog, Inc.	@workingdogsales
(W)right On Communications	@wrightoncomm
Xenophon Strategies	@XenophonPR
Zaria PR	@zaria_pr
Zeno Group	@zenogroup
Zenzi	@zenziPR
Zimmerman Agency	@zimmeranagency
Zimmerman/Edelson, Inc.	@Zimmed
Zoetica Media	@ZoeticaMedia

PR AGENCIES & COMMUNICATIONS CONSULTANTS — PEOPLE

Name	Title	Company	Twitter Handle
Jeanne Alford	Senior Counselor	Alford Communications	@jealford

Hilary Allard	Vice President	The Castle Group	@hallard
Erin Allsman	Public Relations Director	Brownstein Group	@ErinAllsm
Nadja Amireh	CEO	get noticed! communicatio ns	@nadjalina
Gordon G. Andrew	Managing Partner	Highlander Consulting	@gordonand rew
Marina Apperley	President	PIVOT	@marinaapp erley
Rosemarie Ascherl	PR Director	Sonnhalter	@RMasche rl
Louise Ashby	Founder	LAPR	@Louashspe aker
Stephanie Agresta	EVP, Managing Director of Social Media	Weber Shandwick	@stephagres ta
Linda Arroz	Writer/Analyst	Makeover Media	@lindaarroz
Jay Baer	Social Media Strategist, Speaker	Convince & Convert	@jaybaer
Ned Barnett	President	Brand, Ltd.	@nedbarnett
Christine Barney	CEO & Managing Partner	rbb Public Relations	@cmbarney
Katie Barr	Principal Partner	Purrfect PR	@KatiBarr
Tiffany Barranco	Founder	POP! pr + events	@tiffanyb11 6

Joan Barrett	Owner	The Content Factory	@joanieb83
Tina McCormack Beaty	Account Supervisor	Porter Novelli	@tmstrategy
Joe Becker	VP & Group Manager	Ketchum	@jnbblues
Matt Bennett	Director, Digital PR	ProActive Communications	@mattwbennett
Elisabeth Bergoo	PR & Marketing Coordinator	Regal Lager, Inc.	@BettanPR
David Bernknopf	Partner	SplendidVid, LLC	@dbernk
Erika Bitzer	Vice President	Weber Shandwick	@ErikaBitzer
Kristofer Bjorkman	Founder	Mynewsdesk	@ddesk
Candice Blaesing	Owner	ROI Aware	@AdvertisingPR
Ben Blair	Social Media Manager	Crier Communications	@dubblebee
Tamara Bodi	Director of PR and Social Media	McKim Cringan George	@tamara1479
Laurie Pehar Borsh	CEO	Laurie Pehar Borsh PR	@LauriePR
Ashton Bothman	Social Media and Digital Communications Strategist	Juniper Networks	@abothman

Name	Title	Company	Twitter
Amy Bould	Director	Be Bold Media	@amyrb
Chris Brogan	President & CEO	Human Business Works	@chrisbrogan
Derek Brown	Creative Director, Content	JCPR	@JCPRDerek
Stuart Bruce	Principal	Stuart Bruce Associates	@stuartbruce
Quinn Bryner	Account Supervisor	Tierney	@qbryner
Ian Buck	Vice President	High Road Communications	@buckstop
Amanda Burke	Digital Strategist	AxiCom	@AmandaBurke
Johna Burke	Senior VP	BurrellesLuce	@gojohnab
Shonali Burke	Principal	Shonali Burke Consulting	@shonali
William Byrne	Senior Corporate Communications Manager	Digital Kitchen	@WilliamByrne
Idil Cakim	Senior VP	Golin Harris	@idilgh
John Carter	Director	WCG	@jpcarter
Kevin Cary	Public Relations Account Manager	Walker Marketing	@Kevin_Cary
Tina Cassidy	Vice President	Solomon McCown & Co.	@HistoryOfBirth

Celine Castellino	Partner	Copy Creators	@cc363
Elizabeth Castro	Vice President	O'Malley Hansen	@eliz_castro
Rebecca Chappell	Account Executive	(W)right On Communications	@beccachapp
Elyse Charlesworth	Account Coordinator	(W)right On Communications	@ElyseDion
Ashleigh Chatel	Associate	Lambert, Edwards & Associates	@achatel311
David Chauvin	Director of Public Relations	Zimmerman/Edelson, Inc.	@dachauvin
Andy Checo	Account Supervisor	RL Public Relations	@andycheco
Laura A. Clementi	Senior Account Executive	Ketchum	@Laura_Clementi
Steve Cody	Managing Partner & Co-founder	Peppercom	@RepManCody
Carol Cone	Managing Director, Brand & Corporate Citizenship	Edelman PR	@carolcone
Tom Coombes	Founder and CEO	Cognito	@TomC_Cognito
Liza Costandino	Public Relations	Borgata Hotel Casino & Spa	@LizaPeanut

33

	Manager		
Angela Courtney	Owner	Courtney Marketing PR	@courtneympr
Dorothy Crenshaw	CEO	Crenshaw Communications	@dorothycrenshaw
Cheryl Crow	Owner	Via Marketing	@Cheryl_Crow
Jennifer Curley	President	Curley Company	@Jennifer_Curley
Devonne Cusi	PR Coordinator	JCPR	@DevJCPR
Bill Dablec	Senior Vice President	APCO Worldwide	@BillDalbec
Lynda Daboh	Joint Managing Director	First Public Relations	@Lynda_firstpr
Paul Dalessio	Vice President	Fleishman-Hillard	@pauldalessio
Chris Daley	Senior Account Executive	Maroon PR	@ChrisDaley43
Anna Daugherty	The Bugler	Motion Marketing & Media	@thebugler
Douglass Davidoff	Principal Consultant	Straight Talk Group	@dougtweets
Stephen Davies	Consultant	3W PR	@stedavies
David Davis	Strategy Consultant & Managing Partner	Core Strategy & DavisDenny	@dd_iam

Devin Davis	Senior Account Executive	Sterling PR	@DevinDavis
Katelyn Davis	Assistant Account Executive	AxiCom	@katelyndavis
Aliah Davis-McHenry	President and CEO	Aliah Public Relations	@aliahpr
Anna De Souza	President	Live in Five Pubic Relations	@annades
Peter Debreceny	Strategy Execution Consultant	Gagen MacDonald	@PeterDeb
Todd Defren	Principal	SHIFT Communications	@TDefren
Lisa Desatnik	PR Contractor & Consultant		@goodthingslisa
Erik Deutsch	Principal	ExcelPR Group	@ErikDeutsch
John Deveney	Founder	Deveney Communication	@johndeveney
Jackie DiBella	Associate Account Executive	Zimmerman/Edelson, Inc.	@jackie_dibella
Jeff Domansky	CEO	Peak Communications, Inc.	@theprcoach
Kevin Dorrian	Director	Acumen	@kevin_dorrian
Richard Dukas	CEO	Dukas PR	@Rdukas

Imelda	Dulcich	Imelda Dulcich Public Relations	@ImeldaDulcich
Helen Duncan	MD	MWE Media	@HDduncan
Mark Eber	President	IMRE	@IMREIQ
Anna Eschenburg	Social Media Manager	SocialChorus	@aeschenburg
Susan Ennis	President	EnSpire Communication Consultants	@EnSpireSusan
Antonio Erales	Principal	Useful Marketing	@antonioerales
Caitlin Eward	Emerging Media Associate	Calypso Communications	@caitew
Sally Falkow	Social Media Strategist	Meritus Media	@sallyfalkow
Jason Falls	Principal	Social Media Explorer LLC	@jasonfalls
Lori Feldman	President	The Database Diva	@lorifeldman
Werner Fernandes	Managing Partner	Pink & White Consulting LLP	@wernerf
Michael Fineman	Owner	FinemanPR	@michaelfineman
Abbie Fink	Vice President & General Manager	HMA Public Relations	@AbbieF
Laura Finlayson	Vice President	Beckerman PR	@lauramfin
James Finn	SVP,	Twentieth	@finnatfox

	Corporate and PR	Century Fox Home Entertainment	
Chris Floore	Director of Public Affairs	City of Macon	@ChrisFloore
Katie Foley	Senior Account Executive	lotus823	@lotus823_Katie
Patrick Ford	CEO	Burson-Marsteller	@fordpat
Amy Burke Friedman	Vice President	Profiles, Inc.	@amyburke02
Amado Fuguet	Director	Fuguet Comunicacion y Cambio	@Amadofuguet
David Fuscus	CEO and President	Xenophon Strategies	@DavidFuscus
Leslie Gaines-Ross	Chief Reputation Strategist	Weber Shandwick	@ReputationRx
Juergen Gangoly	Managing Partner	The Skills Group	@juergengangoly
Kim Genkin	Executive Partner	The Whole Enchilada PR	@kimgenkin
Amy Gershkoff	Global Director of Analytics	Burson-Marsteller	@amygershkoff
Joe Ghantous	CEO	Right Service	@joehantous
Luke Gibson	Account Executive	Evolve Communications	@oldbaystyle
Leslie	PR Consultant	4GreenPs	@sweetteata

37

Name	Title	Company	Handle
Gilliam			lking
Andy Gilman	President & CEO	CommCore Consulting Group	@agilman
Brian Gluckman	VP, Social & Mobile	The Glover Park Group	@bgluckman
Harry Gold	CEO & Managing Partner	Overdrive Interactive	@HarryJGold
Jenifer Golden	Manage of Agency Operations	H&M Communications	@jenthejew
Carol Kinsey Goman	President	Kinsey Consulting Services	@CGoman
Liz Gorman	Vice President, Corporate Responsibility	Cone	@lizinlfp
Susan Gosselin	Director of PR	Vest Advertisng, Marketing & PR	@sgosselin
Pete Grasso	Account Director	Liggett Stashower	@pgrasso
Tara Greco	Vice President	APCO Worldwide	@TeeGrec
Anne Psolka Green	Junior Writer	JCPR	@AnnaPsolka
Angela Grossfield	Vice President	Porter Novelli	@anggrossfeld
Huma Gruaz	CEO & President	Alpaytac, Inc.	@HumaGruaz
Sarah Gubara	Manager of Social	Maroon PR	@sgubara

Name	Title	Company	Twitter
	& Digital Media		
Steve Gunn	Director	Steve Gunn & Associates	@stevegunn
Eilen Guo	Founder & CEO	Impassion Media	@eileenguo
Allyce Hackmann	Assistant Vice President	JCPR	@AllyceHackmann
Beth Haiken	Senior Vice President	Ogilvy Public Relations Worldwide	@BethHaiken
Scott Hanson	President	HMA Public Relations	@hanner66
Sarah Hardwick	CEO	Zenzi	@SarahZ
Brittany Harmon	Account Coordinator	Vault Communications	@bharm
Victoria Harres	Director, Audience Development	PR Newswire	@VictoriaHarres
Garland Harwood	Account Director	Weber Shandwick	@gharwood
Peter Heffring	President	Expion	@pheffring
Kennetih Hein	Director of Marketing	gyro	@KennethHein
Jodie Heisner	President	Bottomline Media Coaching	@JodieHeisner
Jared Hendler	Executive VP, Global Director:	MWW Group	@jaredhendler

Name	Title	Company	Twitter
	Digital, Social & Creative		
Michael Herman	Chairman & CEO	Communication Sciences International	@mlherman
Jennifer Hesseltine	Co-founder	Sprig Social Media	@jenhesseltine
Allie Herzog	CEO	Integrate PR	@allieherzog
Dean Heuman	Principal and Senior Strategist	Focus Communications	@dheuman
Melissa Hoistion	Senior Account Executive	R&J Public Relations	@mhoistion
Shel Holtz	Principal	Holtz Communication + Technology	@shelholtz
Jordan Hora	Public Relations & Communications	Moroch Partners	@Jordan_JAH
Lisa Horn	Founder	Content Matters	@thepublicitygal
Sabrina Horn	Founder, President and CEO	Horn Group	@sabrinahorn
Heather Horsey	Account Manager	Weise Communications	@HutchH
Diana Hossfeld	Assistant Account	Bread and Butter PR	@DianaTakesaBite

Name	Title	Company	Twitter
Kristina Houck	Executive Research and Online Content Specialist	(W)right On Communications	@KristinaHouck
Kari Hudnell	Media Manager	CommunicationWorks, LLC	@KariLH
Dana Hughens	CEO	Clairemont Communications	@blah2voila
Michele Hujber	Principal	Huber Public Relations	@mlhujber
Ken Hunter	VP, Account Services	R&J Public Relations	@khunter1
Rachel Hutman	Account Executive	Clearpoint Agency	@RachelHutman
Jennifer Huwer	Senior Account Manager	Susan Magrino Agency	@JenniferHuwer
Dave Imre	CEO	IMRE	@daveimre
David Ing	Managing Director	CFA	@davidinguk
Dimitris Ioannides	Communications Consultant	Action Global Communications	@DimitrisI
Quwania J.	President	TSF Marketing & Media	@quwaniahaipr
Al Jackson	Head of CCC DC	Chandler Chicco Companies (CCC)	@CCCHealth2012
Kenny Jahng	CEO	Big Click Syndicate	@kennyjahng
Angela	Vice President,	VMS	@ajeffrey1

Jeffrey	Editorial Research		
Heath Jeliazkov	Principal	Ovation PR	@helijaz
Jocelyn Johnson	CEO	Gravitas Communicatio ns	@jocelynjmj
Karen Johnson	PR Consultant	JAC	@horsewrite r
Madeline	Johnson	The Market Council	@marketcou ncil
Sean Johnson	Public Relations & Social Media Specialist	Weidert Group	@Sean_P_J ohnson
Trevo Jonas	Director of Social Media	Access Communicatio ns	@TrevR
Liza Jones	President	Full Circle PR	@lizapjones
Cheryl Joost	Administrative Assistant	JCPR	@CherylLy nnJoost
Kinetra Joseph	Principal Consultant	Shift Consulting	@KinetraSJ oseph
David Kalson	CEO	Ricochet PR	@kaldak
Wafa Kanan	CEO & Founder	Unique Image Inc.	@wafakana n
Andrea Kavanagh	President	Andera Kavanagh & Associates	@andreahka vanagh
Kathy Keller	Director, Public	Protiviti	@KathyKell erPRO

42

	Relations		
Anne Kennedy	Founder	Beyond Ink	@AnneKennedy
Patrick Kerley	Senior Digital Strategist	Levick Strategic Communications	@pjkerley
Stephanie Kersey	Senior Publicist, Social Media Director	Knock on Wood Communications	@KerseyKnowsBest
Steve Keyser	President	Launch Publicity	@PRprosteve
Rich Klein	President	LawFirmsPR	@RichKleinNY
Leah Knepper	PR Specialist	Rubberneck Media	@leah_tweets
Jody Koehler	Founder	Coopr	@jodykoehler
Tony Kono	Senior Vice President	JCPR	@tonykono
Ashan Kumar	Managing Director	PR WIRE	@ashankumar
Taline Kundakji	Vice President	Marina Maher Communications	@TalineLK
Jillian Kwolek	Vice President	DeVries Public Relations	@jkwolek
Richard Laermer	CEO	RLM PR	@laermer
Sonia LaFountain	Chief Operating	CARMA International	@Sonia_CARMA

43

Name	Title	Company	Twitter
	Officer		
David Landis	President	Landis Communications	@david_landis
Dallas Lawrence	Chief Global Digital Strategist	Burson-Marsteller	@DallasLawrence
Ellen Lebowitz	Publicist	Ellen Lebowitz Press & Publicity	@ellenlebowitz
Gary Lee	CEO	mBLAST	@gary_r_lee
Mitchel Leff	Assistant Account Executive	Kitchen Public Relations	@mitchell_leff
Richard Levick	President & CEO	Levick Strategic Communications	@richardlevick
Cathleen Lewis	Founder	Madison Worldwide	@cathleenlewis
Ian Lipner	Vice President	Lewis PR	@lipneratlewis
Geoff Livingston	Co-founder	Zoetica Media	@geoffliving
Romey Louangvilay	Social Media News-Engine Manager	Euro RSCG Worldwide	@RomeyLouangvila
Stephanie Lough	Account Coordinator	HMA Public Relations	@StephLough
Samantha Luthra	Assistant Account Executive	Bread and Butter PR	@SamanthaLuthra

Monte Lutz	Vice President, Digital Public Affairs	Edelman	@montelutz
Alexander Maasik	CEO	Logios	@AMaasik
Alessandra Malvermi	Managing Partner	Sound Public Relations	@alemal
Ami Manning	President	Volition	@amim
Ronnie Manning	Principal	Mynt Public Relations	@RManning_Mynt
Tim Marklein	Executive VP, Measurement & Strategy	Weber Shandwick	@tmarklein
Saul Markowitz	President	Markowitz Communications	@Pghprman
Georgia Marszalek	Public Relations Counsel	ValleyPR LLC	@ValleyPR
Cyrus Mavalwala	Founder	Advantis Communications	@CyrusMavalwala
Meg McAllister	Managing Director	McAllister PR	@MegmacPR
Cheryl McCants	Principal	Impact Consulting Enterprises	@Cheryl_McCants
Brad McCormick	Executive VP / Global Digital Director	Porter Novelli	@darkbtx
Ashley McCown	President	Solomon McCown &	@AshBoomerSooner

45

Name	Title	Company	Twitter
Vanessa McDonald	VP, Marketing Communications	Co. NATIONAL Public Relations	@VanessaMcD
Mike McDougall	Managing Partner	McDougall Travers Collins	@MikeMcDoug
Ty McKenzie	Public Relations Specialist / CEO	The Elevatyd Experience Group	@Brookale
Mary Ann McQueen	Managing Partner	Authentic PR	@AuthenticPRPro
Lyn Mettler	President	Step Ahead, Inc.	@WebPRGirl
Alyson Miller	Partner	Venture Growth, LLC	@AlysonBMiller
Jessica Miller	Marketing Coordinator	SBC Advertising	@JMillerOC
Lynn Anne Miller	CEO	4GreenPs	@organicmania
Robyn Miller-Tarnoff	PR Consultant	4GreenPs	@TweetnRobyn
Andy Milligan	Co-founder	The Caffeine Partnership	@Caffeinepartner
Nancy Mills	President	The Mills Agency	@NancyVMills
Israel Mirsky	Executive VP, Emerging Media & Technology	Porter Novelli	@israelmirsky

Jennifer Moebius	Principal, Senior Consultant	Moebius Ink	@jennymoebius
Beth Monaghan	Principal	InkHouse Media + Marketing	@bamonaghan
Jack Monson	Vice President	Engage121	@jackmonson
Narelle Morrison	Managing Director	Babel PR	@NarelleMorrison
Monique Moss	Founder	Integrated PR	@moniquemoss
Arti Mulchand	Director	Word of Art	@artiwil
Jon Myers	President	CRUSH PR	@jonmmyers
Michelle Firmbach Nadeau	Founder & Principal	Aqua Communications	@michnadeau
Candice Nicole	CEO	Candice Nicole Public Relations	@candiceNicolePR
Courtney Nolan	Media & Marketing Coordinator	Shirley & Banister Public Affairs	@courtneynolan
John Norris		Moonlight Media Ltd.	@Moonlightlondon
Meg O'Leary	Principal	InkHouse Media + Marketing	@moleary
Fearghal O'Reilly	PR Contractor & Consultant		@fearghaloreilly
Caitrin	Chief of Staff	Burson-	@CaitrinO

47

O'Sullivan	to Pat Ford	Marsteller	
Jenifer Olson	Consultant	JJO Communications	@jenajean
Jeremiah Owyang	Partner & Industry Analyst	Altimeter Group	@jowyang
Louis Pagan	Co-founder & Managing Partner	Hispanicize	@louispagan
Katie Paine	CEO and Founder	KDPaine & Partners	@KDPaine
Katoya Palmer	Owner	ToyBox Consulting	@katoya318
Jamie Pappas	VP, Public Relations & Social Media	AMP Agency	@JamiePappas
Crystal Patriarche	Founder and Publicist	SparkPoint Studio & BookSparks PR	@WriterCrys
Mike Paul	President & Senior Counselor	MGP & Associates PR	@reputationdr
Christine Perkett	Founder	PerkettPR	@missusP
Jonathan Petersen	Social Media Marketing Director	Somersault Group	@jonpetersen
Tracy Pleschourt	Partner & Director of Sustainable Operations	Carmichael Lynch Spong	@tpleschourt

Name	Title	Company	Handle
Stacey Pokluda	Principal	SPPR Consultants	@spokluda
Alina Popescu	CEO	Mirror Communications	@alina_popescu
Bradley Portnoy	Senior Digital Strategist	Weber Shandwick	@bradleyportnoy
CJ Powell	PR Adviser	Cohn Marketing	@CJ_Powell
Amith Prabhu	Account Supervisor - Corporate Affairs	Edelman PR	@amithpr
Angela Prince	Senior Account Director/Principal	A F Prince Associates	@afprince
Sue Procko	President	SPPR, Inc.	@SueProckoPR
Carolyn Prousky	President	CPPR	@CarolynProusky
Theresa Pugh	Director	Communications on TAP	@techyprgirl
Deborah Radman	Senior Counsel	Utopia Communications	@dradman
John Ratcliffe-Lee	Account Supervisor, Digital	MSL Worldwide	@jratlee
Katie Reardon	Senior Associate	Widmeyer Communications	@katiereardon
Sarah Reavis	Corporate Web	FMC	@sarahreavi

49

	Coordinator	Technologies	s
Michal Regunberg	Vice President	Solomon McCown & Co.	@MRintouch
LaNishe Rene	CEO & Sr. Publicist	LR Consulting Enterprise	@LaNisheRene
Blake Rhodes	Vice President	Xenophon Strategies	@BlakeRhodes
Tressa Robbins	Vice President, Media Contacts	BurrellesLuce	@Tressalynne
Paula Roberts	Principal	Humanability	@paulaptr
Gayle Robin	President	Strategic Ampersand	@GRobin
Amy Robinson	Account Manager	Lewis PR	@arobmarie
Ricardo Rodriguez	General Manager	Co+Co	@RicardoRdzO
Rodger Roeser	President & Founder	The Eisen Agency	@eisenthedog
Kaitlin Rogers	Public Relations Manager	Burke Communications	@Kaitlin_PR
Clayton Root	Media Relations Representative	M/C/C	@claytonroot
Patti Rowlson	Marketing Consultant/Publicist	Patti Rowlson Consulting Services	@pattirowlson
Steve Rubel	Executive VP, Global Strategy and	Edelman PR	@steverubel

Name	Title	Company	Handle
Scott Rupp	Insights Co-owner	millerrupp	@scotterupp
Lori Russo	Managing Director	Stanton Communications	@lorirusso
Ron Sachs	President	Ron Sachs Communications	@RonSachsFla
Edgardo Sanabria	Account Executive	The Marketing Source	@esanabria78
Margot Sinclair Savell	Vice President, Measurement & Strategy	Weber Shandwick	@margotsavell
Clinton Schaff	Director, Digital	GolinHarris	@clintschaff
Miriam Schaffer	Account Manager	The Placemaking Group	@Miriam15
Carly Schiff	Account Executive	Pace & Partners, Inc.	@cschiff
Kendra Schultz	Senior Account Executive	HMA Public Relations	@KendraSchultz
Tadd Schwartz	President	Schwartz Media Strategies	@taddschwartz
David Meerman Scott	Marketing Strategist and Author		@dmscott
Steve Seeman	Senior VP & Director of HR	Makovsky + Company	@SteveSeeman
Barbara	President	Barbara Segal	@BabsSegal

Name	Title	Company	Twitter
Segal		& Associates	
Mark Serrano	President	ProActive Communications	@MarkVSerrano
Sophie Sestero	Assistant Account Executive	Ritter Public Relations	@SRSestero
Peter Shankman	Social Media Entrepreneur and Author	HARO	@petershankman
David Sharp	Managing Partner	Sharp Consulting Group	@davidlsharp
Dirk Shaw	Senior Vice President	Ogilvy PR Worldwide	@dirkmshaw
Chancelor Shay	Account Executive	(W)right On Communications	@ChanceShay
Jennifer Shearman	Consultant	Strategic Communications & PR	@jshearmanw
Aileen Shlef	President	Creative Alliance Communications	@AileenRSchlef
Brenda C. Siler	Director	Best Communication Strategies	@bscomm
Doug Simon	President & CEO	DS Simon Productions	@DSSimon
Adam Singer	Social Media Practice Director	Lewis PR	@AdamSinger

Sam Singer	President	Singer Associates	@samsinger
Linette Singleton	Nonprofit Marketing Consultant	Singleton Consulting Group	@scg4nonprofits
Kathy Smith	Public Relations Manager	Simantel Group	@katmsmith
Shaun Smith	Senior Partner, Founder	smith+co	@ShaunSmith_CEM
Abby Snyder	Marketing Specialist	Racepoint Group	@abigailhs
Brian Solis	Principal	Altimeter Group	@briansolis
Helene Solomon	CEO & Co-founder	Solomon McCown & Co.	@HeleneSolomon
Ernesto Sosa	President	SOWEB Inc.	@ernestososa
Geoffrey Stackhouse	Principal	Clarity Solutions	@GeoffStackhouse
Troy Stewart	Marketing Strategist	Snap Design	@troyvstew
Kye Strance	Director of Product Management	Vocus	@KyeStrance
Katie Streater	Representative of Fusion Firm	PRSSA	@katiestreater
Whitney Stringer	Publicist/Social Media Consultant	Whitney Stringer PR & Events	@whitneystringer
Julie Stutzman	Account Associate	Shank Public Relations	@juliestutzman

		Counselors, Inc.	
Heather Sugg	Regional Manager	William Mills Agency	@HeatherSugg
Kaitlyn Sweeney	Senior Account Exec	The Marcus Group	@kpsweeney
Liz Swenton	Director of Operations	March Communications	@lizswenton
Rachel Tabacnic	Account Manager	Fish Consulting	@PRDivaRach
Dana Taormina	Vice President	JCPR	@DanaJCPR
Rik Tiwana	Senior Account Coordinator	Archer>Malmo PR	@riktiwana
Joseph Thornley	CEO	Thornley Fallis	@thornley
Diann Tongco	PR Manager	Dell SonicWALL	@kalindria
Daniel Torchia	Managing Director	Torchia Communications	@dantorchia
Armando Triana	Senior Account Executive	The Marcus Group	@armandotriana
Sherry Treco-Jones	President	Treco-Jones PR	@tjpr
Toby Trompeter	Principal	Trompeter Government Relations & Support Services	@TobyTova

Melanie Trudeau	Marketing Director	Jaffe PR	@Melanie_Trudeau
Ryan Turner	Strategic Communications Consultant	ChangeMatters	@ansinanser
Lars Voedisch	Executive Director	PR.ecious Communications	@larsv
Vicki Voelker	Social Media Coordinator	Gambel Communications	@vickivoelker
Karla Wachter	Senior Vice President	Waggener Edstrom Worldwide	@karlawachter
Ben Wallace	President	Link Positive, Inc.	@BenWallace
Eric Ward	President	EricWard.com	@ericward
Stephanie Watson	CEO	D3P- DZS Promo	@mzsavvypr
Ted Weismann	Senior Vice President	Lois Paul & Partners	@TedWeismann
Jake Wengroff	Global Director of Social Media Strategy & Research Group	Frost & Sullivan	@JakeWengroff
Andy West	Managing Director, Global Client Development	Hotwire PR	@Westofcenter
Heather Whaling	President	Geben Communications	@prtini

55

n

Name	Title	Company	Handle
Hilary White	Director	Hilary White Consulting	@hilwhite1
Bill Whitman	Principal	Whitman & Associates	@bwhitman2
Rachel Wiley	PR Contractor & Consultant		@theRAEreport
Jennifer Williams	Public Relations Director	Williamson and Williams	@williamsjenifer
Lori Williamson	Creative Director	Williamson and Williams	@Curlista
Doug Winfield	Vice President, Digital	MSL New York	@d2k
Jason Winocour	Partner & Digital Media Practice Leader	Hunter Public Relations	@jwinocour
Rebecca Wolfe	Account Executive	AxiCom	@beccawolfe
Ron Wood	President	Ron Wood Public Relations	@woodpr17
Chris Woolford	Account Director	Wolfstar	@ChrisWoolford
Julie Wright	President & Founder	(W)right On Communications	@juliewright
Eric Ziengs	PR Consultant	Geelmuyden-Kiese	@ericziengs
Jordan Zuhr	PR Specialist	Spotlight Communications	@jordanzuhr

CORPORATIONS

Name	Twitter Handle
Adobe	@Adobe
Adobe	@adobepress
Aflac	@aflacduck
AirPac, Incorporated	@AirPacInc
Albania Holidays	@albaniaholidays
Allied Building Products Corp.	@alliedbldgprods
AMD	@amd_unprocessed
American Bankers Association	@ABABankingNews
American Beverage Association	@AmeriBev
American Society of Landscape Architects	@landarchitects
Applebee's	@applebees
Aqua Di Lara	@aquadilara
Associated Press Corporate Announcements	@ap_corpcomm
Associated Press News	@ap
AT&T	@ATT
Bank of America Corp.	@BofA_News
Belk Inc.	@BelkFashionBuzz
Berkshire Hathaway	@BRK_B
Best Buy	@BestBuy
Big Ten Network	@BigTenNetwork
Bloom Solutions	@Bloom_Solutions
Boeing Company	@Boeing
Boingo Wireless	@boingo

Borden Ladner Gervais LLP	@BLGLaw
Borgata Hotel Casino & Spa	@BorgataAC
Bravo	@BravoTV
Brita	@BRITA_PPD
Brocade Communications	@BRCDcomm
Canadian Broadcasting Corporation	@CBC
Cardinal Health	@cardinalhealth
CDS Global	@cdsglobal
Charter Communications	@CharterCom
Chevron	@Chevron
Cisco	@CiscoSystems
Citigroup	@Citi
The Clorox Company	@Clorox
CNN	@CNN
CNN	@CNNPR
Coca-Cola	@CocaCola
Coca-Cola	@CocaColaCo
Comcast	@Comcast
ConocoPhillips	@conocophillips
Costco Wholesale	@CostcoTweets
CPTV	@CPTVOnline
CSC	@CSCNews
Del Monte	@DelMonteFoods
Dell	@Direct2Dell
Dell	@Dell
Dell SonicWALL	@SonicWALL
Deloitte	@Deloitte
Discovery Communications	@DiscoveryComm
Dominion Virginia Power	@DomVaPower
Dow Chemical Company	@dowchemical
drezrehersal Lifestyle LLC	@weplanevents

EdgeLink	@edgelink
Exxon Mobil	@exxonmobil
Fannie Mae	@FannieMae
Firefly Digital	@FireflyGadget
Ford Motor Company	@Ford
Foster Farms	@FosterFarms
General Electric	@generalelectric
General Electric	@GE_Reports
General Motors	@GM
Golfweek Magazine	@GolfweekMag
Gospel Music Channel	@GospelMusicChnl
Green Knack	@GreenKnack
Greene Resources	@GreeneResources
Greenfield Online	@iQuestion
H&R Bock	@HRBlock
Harper's Magazine	@harpers
Heartland Payment Systems	@HPaymentSystems
Heineken	@Heineken_Beer
Heineken	@HeinekenPR
Hewlett-Packard	@hpnews
Hewlett-Packard	@HP
Home Depot	@HomeDepot
Humana	@HumanaHelp
IBM	@IBM_NEWS
Integra Business Systems, Inc.	@paperlessibs
Intuit	@intuit
Jo-Ann Stores, Inc.	@JoAnnStores_PR
Johnson & Johnson	@JNJComm
Juxta Bid	@JuxtaBid

Kerio Technologies	@keriotech
Kimberly-Clark	@KCCorp
Kraft	@kraftfoods
Kroger	@KrogerCo
Lenovo	@lenovo
Lion Brand Yard Company	@LionBrandYard
Lockheed Martin	@LockheedMartin
Lowe's	@Lowes
Macy's	@Macys
Marathon Oil	@MarathonOil
Marriott International, Inc.	@MarriottIntl
Maxim	@Maxim_PR
McKesson	@McKessonCorp
Medifast	@Medifast
Microsoft	@Microsoft
Microsoft	@MSFTnews
MicroStrategy	@microstrategy
Mohegan Sun	@MoheganSun
MTV	@MTV
Nalgene	@NalgeneOutdoor
National Football League	@NFL
National Geographic Channel	@NatGeoChannel
Nationwide Insurance	@Nationwide
NBC Universal	@NBCUniversal
NFL Network	@nflnetwork
Nordstrom	@Nordstrom
NRG EV Services	@nrgenergy
NRG EV Services (eVgo by NRG EV Services)	@evgonetwork
Office Depot	@officedepot
OpenX	@OpenX
Osram Sylvania	@SYLVANIA
Pacific Gas and Electric	@PGE4Me

Panini America	@PaniniAmerica
PepsiCo	@pepsico
PepsiCo	@pepsi
Pfizer	@pfizer_news
PivotGuild	@PivotGuild
Pizza Hut	@pizzahut
Pretty Veggie	@Pretty_Veggie
PRISA DIGITAL Americas	@PDAmericas
Procter & Gamble	@ProcterGamble
Puget Sound Energy	@PSETalk
Quaker Oats	@QuakerOats
Quark	@QuarkXPress
Raytheon Company	@raytheoncompany
Regal Lager, Inc.	@regallager
Rehab Alternatives	@RhbAlternatives
RetailMeNot	@retailmenot
Royal Caribbean	@RoyalCaribbean
SageCircle	@SageCircle
Salesforce.com	@salesforce
Samsung	@Samsungtweets
SAP AG	@sapnews
SAP AG	@SAPNorthAmerica
Sara Lee	@SaraLee_Corp
Sealed Air Corp	@SealedAirCorp
SEGA of America	@SEGA
Shape Magazine	@Shape_Magazine
Shopping Cart Review	@shoppingcartrev
Sodexo, Inc.	@sodexoUSA
Sonic, America's Drive-In	@sonicdrive_in
Sony Electronics	@SonyElectronics

Southwest Airlines	@SouthwestAir
Sprint Nextel	@Sprint
Staples	@Staples
Staples Canada	@StaplesCanada
State Farm Insurance Cos.	@StateFarm
Storenvy	@Storenvy
Target	@Target
Thomson Reuters	@thomsonreuters
Thomson Reuters	@ReutersPR
Time Warner Cable	@TWCable
Travelocity	@travelocity
TuTv	@tutv
United Airlines	@United
United Technologies	@UTC
UPS	@UPS
USANA Health Sciences	@USANAinc
Verizon	@Verizon
VerticalResponse	@VR4SmallBiz
Viacom	@Viacom
Virtualcommodity.net	@netcommodity
Vitera Healthcare Solutions	@viterahealth
Voxiva	@Voxiva_mHealth
Walgreens	@Walgreens
Wal-Mart Stores	@Walmart
The Walt Disney Studios	@DisneyStudios
Wells Fargo	@WellsFargo
Western Union	@WesternUnion
World Wrestling Entertainment	@WWE
Yammer	@Yammer
Yammer	@Yammer_Tips
Zoo New England	@zoonewengland

CORPORATIONS — PEOPLE

Name	Title	Company	Twitter Handle
Dorothy Abernathy	Bureau Chief	Associated Press	@doabernathy
Xochi Adame	AR/PR & Social Media Strategist	CDS Global	@xochiadame
Joe Adams	Public Relations Specialist	Jo-Ann Stores, Inc.	@JoeAdms
Phil Agcaoili	Chief Information Security Officer	Cox Communications	@hacksec
James Aldous	Communications Manager & Consultant	Open X & Freelance	@JamesAldousPR
Holly Allison	Vice President of Marketing	Vico Software	@letsbuildit
Dave Armon	VP, Business Development	Scratch Music Group	@daveyarmon
Maria Baugh	Co-Owner	Butter Lane Cupcakes	@Butterlane
Lara Bersano	PR Associate	PRISA DIGITAL Americas	@larabersano
Ashton Bothman	Corporate Communications Specialist	Brocade Communications	@abothman
B. Bonin	VP, Global	Kraft Foods	@boughb

Name	Title	Company	Twitter
Bough	Digital and Consumer Engagement		
Matt Broder	VP, Corporate Communications	Pitney Bowes	@ctwordsmith
Caroline Bruderer	Director of Public Relations & Communications	Visit Newport Beach, Inc.	@KLinePR
Jennifer Deming Burnham	Group Manager, Content & Social Strategy	Adobe	@adobe
Gina Cali	National Project Tracking Manager	Allied Building Products Corp.	@ginacali
Krista Canfield	Senior Manager, Corporate Communications	LinkedIn	@KristaCanfield
Lou Casale	Corporate PR Director	NCR	@ThePRCurator
Shauna Causey	Head of Social Business	Nordstrom	@ShaunaCausey
Lizette Chavez	Public Relations Director	BlackDivine	@hurricane_liz
Jason	Vice	Harper's	@jasonchup

Chupick	President, Public Relations	Magazine	ick
Kimberly Clark	Lifestyle Producer	drezrehersal Lifestyle LLC	@_Kimberly_Clark
Janette Crawford	Director of Marketing	Storenvy	@janette
Erica Crowder	PR & Marketing Manager	Aqua Di Lara	@EricaDianeC
Bert DuMars	Vice President, E-Business & Interactive Marketing	Newell Rubbermaid	@bwdumars
Tiarra Earis	Policy & Communications Associate	California Partnership to End Domestic Violence	@Sweet_tea85
John Earnhardt	Director, Corporate Communications	Cisco	@urnhart
Frank Eliason	Senior VP of Social Media	Citigroup	@FrankEliason
Jason Forget	Corporate Reputation Manager	GE Energy	@JrFudge
Joel Frey	Senior PR Manager	Travelocity	@cypresswalls
Chris Fuller	Director, PR & Emerging	Pizza Hut	@burbadad

Samantha Garry	Media, U.S. Director, Digital Marketing & Publicity	The Walt Disney Studios	@samanthagarry
Alma Gerxhani	SEO and Online Manager	Albania Holidays	@AlmaGerxhani
Sukhjit Ghag	Social Media Evangelist	Sony Electronics	@sukhjit
Brian Gleason	Director of PR & Social Media Marketing	Medifast	@BGleas
Scott Gulbransen	Director, Social Media & Digital Content	Applebee's	@sdgully
Jay Hamilton	Senior Director - Digital Media, Public Relations	Marriott International, Inc.	@jayhamilton
Amber Harris	Director, Social Media	Discovery Communications	@TheNuwanda
Mary Henige	Director, Social Media & Digital Communications	General Motors Company	@maryhenige
Thomas Hoehn	Director, Interactive	Kodak	@TomHoehn

Name	Title	Company	Twitter
Chris Hotzak	Marketing and Convergence Media Social Media Advisor / Marketing	Rehab Alternatives	@chrishotzak
Phil Hughes	Manager, Product PR	AMD	@AMDPhil
Jim Issokson	Vice President, Corporate Communications	MasterCard	@JimmIssokson
Jennifer L. Jacobson	Director of PR & Social Media	Retrevo	@jcommunication
Michael Jaindl	Chief Client Officer	Buddy Media	@jaindl
Ashley Jang	Public Relations Specialist	Staples Canada	@ashley_jang
Dennis Johnson	Director of Communications	NFL Network	@insidenflmedia
Carly Kade	Communications Specialist	eVgo by NRG EV Services	@CarlyAKade
Dawn Kelly	Vice President, Global Communications	Prudential Financial	@prmaven17
Mark Keys	Vice	WWE	@MarkSKe

Name	Title	Company	Twitter
	President, Content Production & Social Media		ys
Rachel Knight	Account Director	Maxim	@RachelLK
Corinne Kovalsky	Director, Digital & Social Media	Raytheon Company	@corinnekovalsky
Jennifer Kremer	Senior Marketing Manager	Adobe Systems	@jlkremer
Dan Macuga	VP of Marketing, PR & Social Media	USANA Health Sciences	@Dan_Macuga
Frank Mantero	Director, Corporate Citizenship	General Electric	@fmantero
Glenn Manishin	Partner	Duane Morris LLP	@glennm
Cynthia Martinez	Manager, Global Corporate Communications	Royal Caribbean Cruises Ltd.	@CrisisCommChick
Michael McManus	Director, Public Relations	Sodexo, Inc.	@mcmassociates
Christi McNeill	Emerging Media Strategy	Southwest Airlines	@christimcneill

Name	Title	Company	Twitter
	Specialist		
De Anna McPherson	VP, Customer Management	Yammer	@dmcp
Paolina Milana	Executive VP, Global Marketing	Marketwire	@pmilana
Joshua Nafman	Digital Engagement Manager	PepsiCo	@jnafman
Katherine Nelson	VP, Communications	Discovery Communications	@katherinen
Baochi Nguyen	PR & Social Media Manager	Boingo Wireless	@baoch
Kerry Noone	Social Media Manager	CSC	@KerryNoone
Paige Nunn	Manager, Social Media	Dominion Virginia Power	@PaigeNunn
Nick Panayi	Director, Global Brand & Digital Marketing	CSC	@Nickpanayi
Paul Parmley	Social Media Representative	Pacific Gas and Electric	@PaulParmley
Melissa R. Parrish	Analyst	Forrester Research	@melissarparrish
Shane Peck	Senior Communications Coordinator	Parsons Brinckerhoff	@shanepeck
Jeremy Pepper	Director of Public	Palisade Systems	@jspepper

Rich Pesce	Relations Senior Manager, Social Media & Digital Communications	Sprint	@rpesce
Ashley Pettit	Communications Analyst	Southwest Airlines	@ashleypettit
Ilana Rabinowitz	Vice President of Marketing	Lion Brand Yard Company	@Ilana221
Greg Radner	Global Head of PR Services	Thomson Reuters	@radshiz
Scott Rupp	Senior Manager, Public Relations	Vitera Healthcare Solutions	@scotterupp
Holly Ryan	Manager, PR, Marketing & Media	CueSports International	@HollyRyan1
Priya Shah	Social Media Manager	Square Trade, Inc.	@shahpriya
Sanjeev Sharma	Chief Manager, Corporate Communications	Oil and Natural Gas Corporation	@sanjshar214
Michael Smith	Partner	Borden Ladner Gervais LLP	@MichaelSmithYYZ
Andrew Staples	PR Manager	Kerio Technologie	@andrew_kerioPR

s

Name	Title	Company	Twitter
Esther Steinfeld	Public Relations Manager	Blinds.com	@EstherSteinfeld
Heidi Sullivan	Vice President, Media Research	Cision	@hksully
Brooks Thomas	Emerging Media Coordinator	Southwest Airlines	@brooksethomas
Scott Townsend	Marketing Director	United Linen & Uniform Services	@UnitedLinen
David Tra	Social Media Specialist	Discovery Communications	@dtra
Autumn Truong	Senior Social Media Strategist	Cisco	@autumntt
Evan Welsh	Global Media Relations Lead	SAP AG	@evwelsh
Kristin Wertz	Corporate Social Responsibility	Pizza Hut	@KLWertz
James Wisdom	2nd Vice President, Integrated Marketing	Aflac	@wisdom
Christi Woodworth	Director of External	Sonic, America's	@cwoodworth

Communicatio Drive-In ns

I warned you it was extensive and complete so use it wisely. Now let's discuss the insider secrets to obtaining celebrity endorsements and then I will show you how to make contact with celebrities and their representatives.

Chapter 2 – Insider Secrets to Obtaining Celebrity Endorsements

What I am going to teach you now is worth its weight in gold.

Stars and celebrities have rankings such A-grade stars (Jennifer Lopez, Justin Bieber, Oprah Winfrey, etc). Here is a list of A-grade stars:

1. Will Smith
2. Johnny Depp
3. Brad Pitt
4. Tom Hanks
5. George Clooney
6. Will Ferrell
7. Reese Witherspoon
8. Nicolas Cage
9. Leonardo DiCaprio
10. Russell Crowe

Then you have B-grade stars – go here:

http://www.rottentomatoes.com/quiz/bgrade-movie-stars-can-you-name-them/

Their grade will determine the fee they charge to endorse. Be careful; before Tiger Woods downfall from grace, Nike paid him over $20-million/year for his endorsement.

There are many tools small businesses can use to evaluate celebrity appeal. These include the following:

Q Score - http://www.qscores.com/Web/Index.aspx
E-Score   -
http://www.epollresearch.com/corp/products/escoreCelebrity.view
Nielsen   Media   reports   -
http://www.nielsen.com/us/en/reports/2012/state-of-the-media-the-social-media-report-2012.html
Forbes 100 list - http://www.forbes.com/celebrities/list/
Google Fight - http://www.googlefight.com/

There are government guidelines when dealing with endorsements. Go here for The FTC's Revised Endorsement Guides:

http://www.business.ftc.gov/documents/bus71-ftcs-revised-endorsement-guideswhat-people-are-asking

Celebrities have been known to endorse some pretty whacky things. Check this out:

http://funny-pictures.feedio.net/celebrity-leverage/celebrityleverage.com*wp-content*uploads*2010*01*stop_upsell.png/

There are different type of endorsements and different costs associated with these endorsements. By far, telephone interviews are the least expensive of endorsements and they require that you send an advance list of questions and do not deviate from these questions. These types of endorsements are best for radio, podcasts, book writing, etc.

Any type of endorsement that requires filming and/or location shots will be the most expensive. In between is everything from meetups to static photo endorsements.

Again, matching the star to the product/service is critical.

Another site that you will find useful is HARO: http://www.helpareporter.com/.

I have used this site for years; I am labeled an expert in publishing and forensic science since I run ForensicsNation.com.

I do interviews almost every day of the week and all of them from this one site. When stars are evaluating your product/service, they will check HARO to find out about you so use this site; it is free!!

You can also use HARO to get experts to interview. They may not be stars but they are experts and generally do not charge. When I do an interview I only require that my books for that particular subject be mentioned.

Okay, now I will show you how to make contact with stars and celebrities...

Chapter 3 – Where to Find Celebrity Contact Information

Making contact with stars/celebrities requires diligence and patience especially if you are dealing with their publicist, agent or representative. They can be and most of the time is a pain in your backside!!!

First, here is a Fiverr.com person that actually does a daman fine job in getting you contact info and for a small price of $5.

http://fiverr.com/benm722/find-celebrity-contact-information

Here is an extensive list of contact resources:

- **FanMail.biz**
  Find contact information for your favorite actor,

actress, director, model, singer, sports player, or music group.
www.fanmail.biz
- **Stars Autographs**
Includes a list of celebrity autographs and emails and street addresses. Also offers pen pals worldwide.
www.autographsuccess.com
- **CelebritiesFans.com**
Offers a large, searchable database of celebrity home and email addresses, photographs, and other memorabilia items.
www.celebritiesfans.com
- **Write To a Celeb**
Mailing addresses of celebrities.
www.writetoaceleb.com
- **Seeing Stars: Celebrity Mailing Addresses**
Searchable database of addresses.
www.seeing-stars.com/Search.shtml
- **New York Stars Map**
Interactive streetmap to the celebrities' homes in New York. In Flash and available in PDF format as well.
www.nymag.com/news/people/18842/index4.html
- **CelebrityAddys.com**
www.celebrityaddys.com

1. **Find them on a social media network or on a legitimate website**. Finding one of the following is an important first step in contacting celebrities. Make sure that the website is frequented by the actual celebrity, not their agent, publicist or an

impersonator. The following fall in order of "most likely to contact" to "least likely to contact the celebrity."

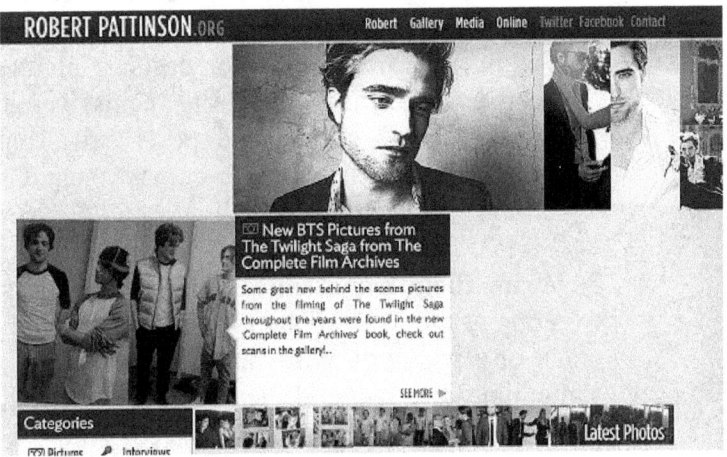

o   **Twitter: Look for "tweets" that are posted by the celebrity.** These tweets should be directed back at people who "tweeted @" the celebrity, that have actual photos of the celebrity that are taken in real life (not a studio or "official" portfolio photos), or "tweets" that are written about daily experiences of the celebrity. These are all good signs that you can "tweet @" the celebrity to actually contact them.

o   **Their "Official" Website: Celebrities** almost always have "Official websites" that they promote. This means you have a chance of being able to contact them via this method. While it's not preferred, since usually these are "managed" by publicists or agents, this can be a way to contact them. Search the site for actual responses to fan mail. If you can't find them, move on.

o   **Facebook:** Most Facebook accounts are "managed" by someone other than the celebrity. Again, you are looking for posts or pictures that seem to be from the celebrity themselves. If only "professional" photos and posts exist, this isn't going to be the best way to contact them. Chances are this will be the case.

2. **Write them a message.** Whether the message is tweeting at them, a private message to their inbox, an email or a post, you will want to spend time to write something original and heart-felt or funny, which make you more likely to get noticed. Find a balance between being too lengthy and too short, both of which are likely to get overlooked.

Your Name (required)

Jane

Your Email (required)

jane@email.com

Subject

Hi Rob|

Your Message

Hello, I think you are amazing and I love all your movies! xx

Send

3. **Wait for a reply.** Depending on the celebrity, they may be getting dozens to thousands of messages a day. This means they will need time to shift through and find yours.

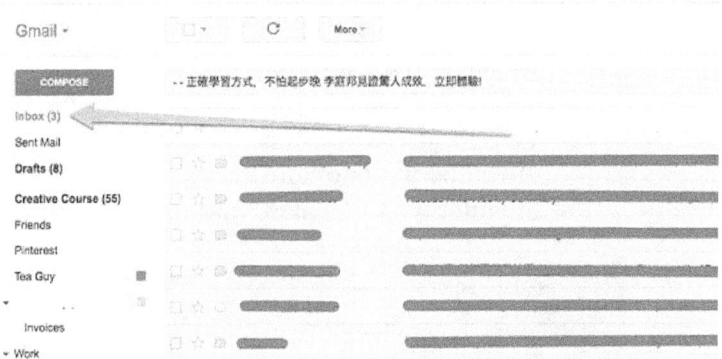

4. **Find an address.** Sometimes addresses for fan mail are available on the "Official Websites" of celebrities. If that is not the case, you can find this information by Googling "Fan Mail + [celebrity name]."

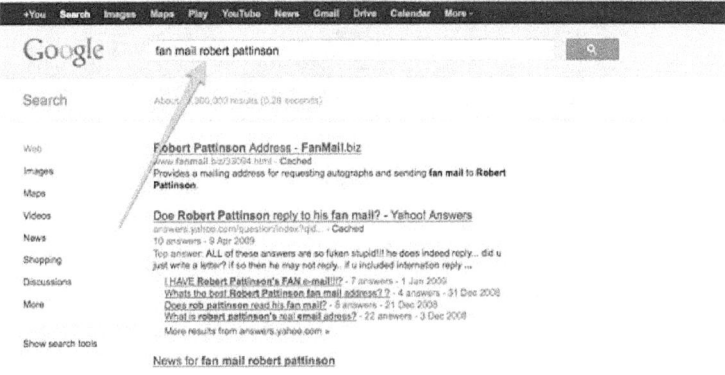

5. **Write a letter.** You will want to spend time to write something original and heart-felt or funny, which make you more likely to get noticed.

    o   Include something to autograph. Enclose a photo of the celebrity or a cover of a magazine the celebrity was on for them to sign and send back.
    o   Include a pre-paid return envelope with your address/information. Make sure that this envelope has enough stamps to return a letter plus anything you included for autographing.

6. **Wait for a response.** Depending on the celebrity, they may be getting dozens to thousands of messages a day. This means they will need time to shift through and find yours.

Tips

•   Pay attention to where you are sending online letters. Many people post letters to celebrities on random websites. They don't confirm the site belongs to the celeb or their agent.

•   Look at the URL (address) of the page. If it's not JUST the celebrity, agency, or studio's name (not JohnnyDeppPersonalWebsite.com, for example) it's probably not actually their site.

•   Celebrities often change their agencies. The addresses you find on the Internet or in books may be out-of-date in a few months.

•   Politely request a personalized message. This will mean more to you in the long run and may also help you avoid getting an autograph that has been signed by autopen rather than by the person. The downfall is that personalized autographs lower the value of the picture.

•   If you have legible handwriting, handwrite your letter for a personal touch. It shows you put some effort into it and you're not using a form letter.

•   Write "Forwarding Service Requested" under the destination or return address and the Post Office will hopefully forward your letter to the celebrity's current address.

•   Don't ask for more than one or two autographs at a time or send more than two photos. This will show the celebrity that you are a collector and not, perhaps, a real fan.

•   Be warned that online messages are not likely to get through to a celeb. Think how easy it is to write online, then think of how many people are probably doing it, and how much time someone would have to spend to answer everything.

•   Don't say that you are collecting autographs or that you're a collector. Celebrities are generally happier to give autographs to fans than to collectors.

•   Don't give generic compliments. Mention things such as a specific movie the star appeared in, a specific character he or she played, your favorite song by the star, or a great play they made in a baseball game. You'll seem like a true fan.

• Sometimes they have what's called an "agency" - some of the time might be doing all the fan mail reply rather than have the celebrity do it. Like pretending to be the celebrity answering all the letters. Keep that in mind.

• Your letter will probably be seen by a lot of people, so don't say anything too personal or embarrassing. Personal details discourage agents from passing your letter on. Don't tell them you love them or you want to marry or have "fun" with them.

• If you want to be unique when sending a letter in the mail, decorate it! Think about it, if you where them, which letter would you open first. The plain white one or the one with stickers on it and cool decorations on it?

Warnings

• Do not pay for contact with a celebrity. There are many online services which claim they can put you in touch with celebrities if you pay a fee. These are scams.

• Don't call, continually pester, or stalk a celebrity. If you don't get a reply after one or two letters, stop. Repeated or rude requests are annoying at the very least and can constitute harassment or stalking in more serious cases.

• Writing "Forwarding service requested" on the envelope may cause you to incur additional fees from the Post Office.

Sources and Citations

• ContactAnyCelebrity.com Contains contact information for 67,300+ celebrities worldwide

• AutographSuccess.com Another collecting site with tips and a forum

• Alex's Autographs.com A baseball autograph collector's site

• CelebrityHangout.co.uk UK autograph collecting resource

• FanMailAddresses.com The website for the Star Directory.

• IMDB.com The Internet Movie Database. Searchable, with profiles of movie stars, photos, and (for subscribers) contact information

• StarTiger A large celebrity address database and autograph collector community

• Star-Collector.net Large address database including mailing and email. Updated conventions page

• Twitter Now the biggest website where many celebrities turn to for short updates for a more interactive conversation online.

• TheHandbook.com A database with over 30,000 celebrity agents, managers and publicists details.

Here is a paid site with a pretty extensive database:

http://contactanycelebrity.com/join/?utm_expid=1874105
5-
16&utm_referrer=http%3A%2F%2Fwww.contactanycele
brity.com%2Ffree%2F

http://contactanycelebrity.com/trial/do/celebrityList

Chapter 4 – Celebrity Look-Alikes

FaceDouble

Ranking: 7.95
Vote

Angelina Jolie
Jane Smith in Mr. & Mrs
Smith (2005)

In actuality, I use lookalikes more than actual celebrities. People respond the same as if the celebrity is real even if they don't know the lookalike is not the real celebrity.

In one of my events I brought in a half dozen lookalikes and one real star. I then ran a contest for the attendees to pick the real star from the lookalikes. Not once did they pick the real star. It was quite fun and went over gangbusters with my attendees.

Check out these lookalikes:

http://www.wetpaint.com/network/gallery/double-take-wetpaint-entertainment-stars-celebrity-lookalikes-

Here is a search engine for lookalikes:

http://www.picitup.com/NewMatch/

Go here to book lookalikes:

http://www.looktwice.com/
http://www.gigsalad.com/Impersonators-Tributes/Impersonators-Lookalikes
http://www.scarlettentertainment.com/walk-around-act/look-a-like
http://www.royaltalent.com/Impersonators.htm
http://www.costelloentertainments.co.uk/3770/8/artists/-celebrity-lookalikes.aspx
http://www.lookalikes.info/

Now I need you to put on your Marketing Thinking Cap to determine how to best use celebrity lookalikes/impersonators. I gave you one example of how I used impersonators but when you think about it, there are tons of ways to use them and they are considerably cheaper than the real stars!!!

Now I want to discuss is it really worth using celebrity endorsements or not. Read on…

Chapter 5 – Would a celebrity endorsement of a product influence your decision to purchase that product?

This is a million-dollar question!!! And one that deserves looking into in detail. First, go here and check this out:

http://www.sodahead.com/entertainment/would-a-celebrity-endorsement-of-a-product-influence-your-decision-to-purchase-that-product/question-2086955/?link=ibaf&q=would%20a%20celebrity%20endorsement%20of%20a%20product%20influence%20your%20decision%20to%20purchase%20that%20product

Here is an article well worth reading:

How Much Influence Do Celebrity Endorsements Really Have on Our Purchasing Decisions?

Written by Jill Ettinger
http://www.organicauthority.com/sanctuary/how-much-influence-do-celebs-really-have-on-our-purchasing-decisions.html

News that superstar Beyoncé is going to receive $50 million for doing Pepsi advertisements (including a performance at the 2013 Super Bowl Half Time Show) sent food and health advocacy groups into a frenzy—how could this new mother lend her support to one of the biggest factors in our nation's obesity epidemic? Doesn't she have any ethics? A Grammy-award winning performer—and wife of rapper/mogul Jay-Z—certainly Beyoncé isn't hurting for the cash, either. Besides, will her celebrity endorsement in a Pepsi ad even sell more products, anyway?

The short answer: Yes. But, it's actually a lot more complicated.

We are no strangers to celebrities selling us lots of things. Brad Pitt has recently been appearing in Chanel commercials (as if anything smells better than Brad's man-odor). His wife, Angelina Jolie, has pushed Louis Vuitton. His ex-wife (Jennifer Aniston) was the face of Glaceau's Vitamin Water. Burger King unveiled its recent healthy menu changes with help from celebs including Steven Tyler, Salma Hayek and soccer player David Beckham—a superstar athlete hocking fast food? Really? When Dr. Oz mentions omega-fatty acids, store shelves are empty for days. When he came under attack for his December 2012 TIME magazine article in which he seemed to dismiss organic food, echoes of "Yah! Organic food is too expensive!" could be heard from every corner of the Internet, and outrage at his comments from every other corner—as if his words were etched in slabs of stone.

According to a University of Arkansas research study (in conjunction with Manchester Business School in the United Kingdom), the reason we see so many celebrities in product advertisements and endorsement situations may be that marketers are keenly aware that "a range of consumer-celebrity relationships conspires to allow consumers to form a personal identity that matches who they want to be." These messages (which can be multiple ads for one product/brand from a celebrity, or even multiple different brands that rely on the same celebrity), "help consumers develop a portfolio of relationships that allow them to function as creators of meaning for themselves." The study authors call these relationships "celebrityscapes" or "celebrity bricolages." In other words, if you eat/smoke/drink the same as David Beckham or Brad Pitt, you might also think you emulate their other (mega) more desirable traits, too. In the case that you don't want to emulate them, but rather are attracted to them, you're still more likely to purchase those products in some strange psychological attempt to attract that (type of) person into your life. (That is TOTALLY NOT why I would buy anything Brad Pitt's worn or accidentally grazed.) It's a little bit magic...yes, but mostly just misspent money.

As a culture that spends much of our free time in front of the television and/or movie screen, celebrity endorsements are paramount to a brand's success—especially as consumers are becoming better educated and more aware about what food and products they're purchasing. A consumer's predilection for celebrities will make them more sympathetic to a brand—even one that's been pinpointed as causing our nation's health problems. If our favorite movie star is munching on a KitKat bar, they probably know something we don't, right? (They do: the exact number of zeroes on their endorsement check.)

A Taiwanese study found that consumers are quicker to "memorize" the product a celebrity is involved with, whether they're a fan or not. The human brain recognize celebrities similarly to how we recognize people we actually know. This tethers us to whatever they're promoting. And if we happen to be fans, we're even more likely to place value on products they're endorsing—just like advice from a valued friend.

Back in the 1920s, advertising genius Bruce Barton, who helped create the brand that is General Electric, said that branding helps corporations "find their souls" and become more real, more important to the consumer. As the bright labels and sleek ads of branded products overshadowed boring old commodities, celebrities naturally fell into the delivery mechanism in earnest. With industry finding its footing, and many companies still privately-owned and operated at the beginning of the 20th century, this model made sense. Those celebrities were more likely to use the products they promoted, feed them to their families and friends. But do you really think David Beckham regularly eats at Burger King? What about Beyoncé? How many Pepsis will she likely drink today?

Of course, a celebrity doesn't have to be alive to sell products, either. Scores of ads have relied on celebrities from bygone eras. Many simply use a popular song by a popular artist, or feature a cartoon or comic book character to infuse an emotional attachment with the audience. In her seminal 1999 best-selling book, *No Logo: Taking Aim at the Brand Bullies*, Naomi Klein wrote, "By the end of the 1940s, there was a burgeoning awareness that a brand wasn't just a mascot or a catchphrase or a picture printed on the label of a company's product; the company as a whole could have a brand identity or a "corporate consciousness." This endeavor moved advertisers away from the brands attributes and "toward a psychological/anthropological examination of what brands mean to the culture and to people's lives."

But that methodology may soon be a practice of the past. Blind faith is beginning to wane as consumers are now easily armed with mobile phone apps and a multitude of tools to help them validate products and services, despite what Brad Pitt's wearing. (Seriously though, what is he wearing *right now*? Do you know?) Is it safe? Are there healthier/cheaper/better alternatives? Additionally, cause-driven marketing has skyrocketed in recent years as consumers yearn to make purchasing decisions that "signal a deeply held belief and a profoundly social act," according to *AdAge*, "Brands that understand this and can create a consumer experience that feels less transactional and more pro-social will build deep loyalty."

In a *Fast Company* article, Morgan Clendaniel writes: "Brands that are perceived as irresponsible or just creating products with no meaning are in danger of being severely punished by consumers." Of course that means that the celeb-reliant brands will push even harder to win you over with your favorite stars; brands will also begin selling you on product attributes—the very focus the marketing industry moved away from in the 1940s, because those values, while they may have disappeared for the last half-century, are certainly on the rise. And If a brand *can't* do that—if a company can't tell you why a product is actually good or useful—and if the ads rely instead on sexy actors, cute cartoon characters or popular musicians, chances are that's all that's really being sold to you anyway—a flashy, expensive and fleeting performance. Remember to applaud.

Keep in touch with Jill on Twitter @jillettinger

Now you have both pro and con arguments. You decide based on budget, product/service and price points or profitability.

Chapter 6 – Summary & Conclusion

Okay let's summarize what we have learned.

Using celebrity endorsements offers just as many pros as it does cons. Special care is needed to outline a concise business –type plan in order to ensure that all aspects of celebrity endorsements are covered and the business owner knows exactly what his/her costs will be in advance.

I have gone to great lengths to describe how I have sued celebrity endorsements but also give you specific points to follow as well as what not to do.

I also provided you with the ability to contact celebrities and the different tools available to make it easier in making contact.

In the section describing celebrity lookalikes I offered an alternative to th high cost of using celebrities and I think you will find this section just as rewarding once you implement what I offered and once you design different marketing campaigns that will use lookalikes like the example I gave you.

In the last section, "Would a celebrity endorsement of a product influence your decision to purchase that product?" I attempted to get you to consider the viability and profitability of using celebrity endorsements.

I sincerely hope you enjoyed my presentation. Again, if you have any questions please feel free to write to me: lee.benton@epubwealth.com.

Now I have a special gift for you…read on.

I Have a Special Gift for My Readers

I appreciate my readers for without them I am just another author attempting to make a difference. If my book has made a favorable impression please leave me an honest review.   Thank you in advance for you participation.

My readers and I have in common a passion for the written word as well as the desire to learn and grow from books.

My special offer to you is a massive ebook library that I have compiled over the years. It contains hundreds of fiction and non-fiction ebooks in Adobe Acrobat PDF format as well as the Greek classics and old literary classics too.

In fact, this library is so massive to completely download the entire library will require over 5 GBs open on your desktop.

Use the link below and scan all of the ebooks in the library. You can select the ebooks you want individually or download the entire library.

The link below does not expire after a given time period so you are free to return for more books rather than clog your desktop. And feel free to give the link to your friends who enjoy reading too.

I thank you for reading my book and hope if you are pleased that you will leave me an honest review so that I can improve my work and or write books that appeal to your interests.

Okay, here is the link…

http://tinyurl.com/special-readers-promo

PS: If you wish to reach me personally for any reason you may simply write to mailto:support@epubwealth.com.

I answer all of my emails so rest assured I will respond.

Meet the Author

Dr. Leland Benton is Director of Applied Web Info, a holding company for ePubWealth.com, a leading ePublisher company based in Utah. With over 21,000 resellers in over 22-countries, ePubWealth.com is a leader in ePublishing, book promotion, and ebook marketing.

As the creator and author of "The ePubWealth Program," Leland teaches up-and-coming authors the ins-and-outs of today's ePublishing world. He has assisted hundreds of authors make it big in the ePublishing world.

Leland also created a series of external book promotion programs and teaches authors how to promote their books using external marketing sources.

Leland is also the Managing Director of Applied Mind Sciences, the company's mind research unit and Chief Forensics Investigator for the company's ForensicsNation unit. He is active in privacy rights through the company's PrivacyNations unit and is an expert in survival planning and disaster relief through the company's SurvivalNations unit.

Leland resides in Southern Utah.

Visit some of his websites

http://www.AddMeInNow.com
http://www.AppliedMindSciences.com
http://www.AppliedWebInfo.com
http://www.BookbuilderPLUS.com
http://www.BookJumping.com
http://www.EmailNations.com
http://www.EmbarrassingProblemsFix.com
http://www.ePubWealth.com
http://www.ForensicsNation.com
http://www.ForensicsNationStore.com
http://www.FreebiesNation.com
http://www.HealthFitnessWellnessNation.com
http://www.Neternatives.com
http://www.PrivacyNations.com
http://www.RetireWithoutMoney.org
http://www.SurvivalNations.com
http://www.TheBentonKitchen.com
http://www.Theolegions.org
http://www.VideoBookbuilder.com

www.ingramcontent.com/pod-product-compliance
Lightning Source LLC
Chambersburg PA
CBHW051812170526
45167CB00005B/1989